Scharleen,
Thank you for
being one of my biggest fans?
encouraging me to write!

Love,
Susie Clevenger
2023

# Praise for Susie Clevenger's Work:

For *Dirt Road Dreams*:

"I loved this book. It resonates with harsh truth and gritty reality as it takes the reader on a roller coaster ride named 'Life'."
~ Fiona Marshall

"Susie Clevenger's poetry touches the heart with beauty and depth in her first poetry collection, Dirt Road Dreams. With precision and tenderness, each poem delivers satisfaction; and not one word is wasted."
~ Laurie Kolp, author of *Upon the blue Couch*

For *Insomnia's Ink*:

"...Be the light for another until you've burnt the darkness from alone..." is a powerful line from this book of poetry. Sweeping thoughts leap from each page. The verses speak of the humanity in all of us and our obligation to help those who need it most.
~ James William Peercy, author of *Without A Conscious*

"Susie Clevenger is a seasoned poet, writing with all the force of years behind her. I have probably read this book three or four times already (to be honest, I've lost count). There is a high mastery of structure and emotion in her verse from which the reader cannot easily escape."
~ Ben Ditmars, author of *Sleeping With Earth*

# Where Butterflies Pray

## Susie Clevenger

*Wings O' Butterfly*

Cover Design by Jaqueline E. Smith

Cover Photography by Tim Malek

# Table of Contents

Sunrise
Deeper Blue
A Hymn Note
New Wings of Amnesty
Four O'clock
Collecting Silhouettes
Bits of the Moon
Twilight
Hunger for Illumination
Answer Night
Dream Scent
Mother Moon
Night
Only So Many Lyrics
Whippoorwill Song
When Shadows Grow Bold

## Weeds and Blooms

A Day of Weeds
Weeds into Whimsy
Dandelion Strong
Flight of a Bouquet
Beauty in Gray Sky Concrete
Morning Glories
Wild Rose
A Jasmine Moment
Difference Dandelions and Love
Weed
Knowing when to Bloom

## Spirit

The World in Three Acres
Footprint Memory
Tempest
Goddess of Small Things
Someone up There
Until I Am Cleansed of Noise
Home Has Found Me

# Introduction

Nature has always been my place of confession, comfort, and joy. I have often called it my tabernacle in the wild. It is there I feel most connected to a divine presence. Butterflies represent freedom and transformation. I think of them as winged spiritual guides. From my earliest years I have been drawn to them. Also in this collection are several poems with dandelion references. The dandelion was the first flower I picked as a child; the first bouquet I gave my mother. I have always had a spiritual kinship with it. That yellow weed taught me the joy of giving and overcoming odds to grow in adversity.

*Where Butterflies Pray* is poetry inspired by a higher power, God, the divine I see manifested through nature.

## Dedication

"Now I see the secret of the making of the best person. It is to grow in the open air, and to eat and sleep with the earth."
~ *Walt Whitman*

This is dedicated to my father, Oron Crouch. He instilled in me as a child a deep love and connection to nature.

# Seasons

# Box of Crayons

Roots sing through
broken limbs,
leaves too young to open,
and sparrows gathering
twigs from dying winter.

Venerable oak
write another season
into their journal of rings.

Elder and newborn
drink raindrops from
a gray pitcher sky.

Faithful Spring kneels before
her box of crayons
to search for the perfect
shade of green.

## At Mother Nature's Breast

I see the blossoms of spring
painting the sepia landscape
with bursts of color....
and arguments about
God and evolution disappear.
I can feast at the breast
of Mother Nature's glory
without confessing sin
or faith in theories.

# Frogs of Spring

Spring comes in the croaking of frogs.
Their song of courtship fills the night
chasing away the silence of winter.

Within the throaty call I hear
my childhood along a muddy creek bank
chasing daydreams through newborn grass.

It is odd what stirs the heart to return
to a time when there was as much pain as joy.
Perhaps I needed to be shown I no longer fear the shadows.

Sitting in the rewind I am lost in a time of dreaming,
believing every secret remained untold, and when
life was brand new with no scuff marks of disappointment.

Sing each prince in puddle and pond your courtship song,
I wish you well in your ballroom decorated with spring.
Thank you for mixing my yesterdays with the joy of renewal.

# Elysium

On my knees, hands covered with dirt
I separate weeds from blossoms
until I feel the sigh of done sing in unison
with the wren song of nesting.

Hypnotized by the glory of spring
my eyes feast on purple hyacinths,
yellow daffodils, and coral tulips
declaring winter gray is out of season.

Black robed crows chatter on the tree limbs
above me about Eve's garden delivering apples,
but there are no words of sin in my Elysium.

# Sing of Raindrops

Sing of raindrops
painting spring
on your kitchen window.

Let harmony spill
into the anger
you nurse each sunrise.

Healing is a journey
of a thousand setbacks,
a salted desert formed from tears.

It feels easier to nurse the dragon
than clean the nest you've built
with justifications for venom.

Forgiveness is freedom.
It unties the knot that binds
you to an open wound.

Sing of raindrops bringing spring
to every shadowed place in your spirit
you've surrendered to cruelty's winter.

## Soul Response

A lone daffodil
sprouts sunshine
in the garden.
I mark another
day off winter's
calendar,
and whisper
thank you to
Persephone.

My soul responds
to the earth song
of warmer days.

## Spring's Pillow

She rests her head
on spring's pillow
and dreams of
resurrection.

Tulips stir in their tomb.

## Guilt Is Persistent

Spring Easter eggs the calendar
with resurrection...I confess
my sleeping dogs, then light
another candle praying its wick
will burn another hole in forgetting.

Guilt is a persistent thing.
With photographic memory
it plants my errors among
daffodils and prods me to
pick bouquets and ink notes to God.

## Anointed Sunrise

Each summer morning
I walk my garden
to see if God has bloomed
in lavender, and anointed sunrise
with the glory of peace.

## Blades of Verse

The earth writes
its poems on
blades of grass.

Kneel upon
its sonnets
and breathe
in their verse.

# Sunburnt July

The bay splashes me
with mirrored water
until my daydreams
surrender to the waves.

Reality is too cold under
the sunburnt July sky.

Why swirls above me
with the seagulls and
for a few moments
I don't care there
isn't an answer.

## Summer Embroidery

Summer embroiders
sunflowers in grass,
heat stitched in yellow and green.

Their bowed heads bring
thoughts of prayer.

I wonder if God remembers my voice.

## Sweet Tooth Season

In the sweet tooth season my family's iron skillet
transformed into a raisin black moon
dusted with sugared apple stars.

A song of grandmothers' sang through my mother's spoon
in cinnamon dust notes and yellow butter sun
until the melody of ancestors would reach the final note,
"enough."

Apple scented thoughts of ladder climbs
to reach heavy fruited limbs, wicker baskets, harvest,
promised growling tummies honest labor brought rewards.

On the crescendo of giggle questions mother
extinguished the sun beneath our iron skillet moon,
and dropped apple blessings into bowls even heaven wished to
taste.

# Disciple of Autumn

When death demands its due
let me die as the death of autumn.
She doesn't go quietly or dimly.
The north wind tears at her limbs,
but she bends without breaking.

With glory stolen from the sun
she drops leaves of red and gold
on shorter days gathered on her doorstep.

She is harvest, thanksgiving, the comforter
to spirits walking the valley of mortality.

I want to be a disciple of autumn,
spread her gospel of riotous dying.
My flesh one day will succumb
to the reaper, but my spirit will join
the soil of another soul's evolution.

# Bright Apple Cider Days

Oh October, you like to tease,
dress in bright apple cider days
painted orange, red, and yellow.

When I converse with you I ignore the signs
of the browning to come; the bleak bones
you will leave to tattoo blue sky.

Walking through your rattle whispers
I pretend winter can't freeze your
swaying dance or drain the festival from your cheeks.

October, we are spirit sisters dressed
in sun flames collecting moments
ice can never steal or dull into lead penciled memories.

## Patience

Bare winter trees are dressed
in yellow finch wings
powdered with snow flakes.

With a sigh I draw tulips
on my frosted kitchen window.

Nature opens its lesson plan
to a single word....Patience.

## Quilted Summer

I quilted summer and hung
its sunflower colors on the wind,
a rebellious flag defying winter's gray.
Strips of cloth summon memories
of beaches, ice cream, joy.

Sassy July makes me smile
as I watch it slap the cheek
of a cranky January day.

Dreaming outside the ice
and a little closer to the sun
my thoughts walk serenity's path
of sand, blue sky, thanksgiving.

## Chasing Angels

Snow covers the ground,
a pristine journal
waiting for my footprints
to write memories.

I lift my booted foot
hesitant to mar wonderland.
There is so much ink in a first step.

I am surrounded by breadcrumb
thoughts leading me back home,
my father's steps breaking a path,
frosted mittens, the chill demanding
hot chocolate, the echo of giggles.

Not sure what my boots will write,
the horizon looks so much like the past.
Perhaps I'll just leave a note,
"I was here, sunlit, and chasing angels."

# Trees

38

# Language of Leaves

As still as my bones will allow,
I sit beneath an elm tree
and listen to the language of leaves.
In the wind rustle I hear joy,
rebirth, wisdom, and veins pulsing life.

Within me I feel the dark wounds
I'd nursed begin to tendril toward light.
Wrapped in unity with the tree truth speaks…
"Healing will bud when I stop feeding it agony."

# In The Shadow of a Chinaberry Tree

Hunger came to the wetlands
behind my wrought iron fence
with wild doe eyes searching
my soul to find trust.

Her world of meadows
guarded by tall pines
had disappeared into concrete
and the roar of humans.

In a universe turned enemy
she had followed the sparrow song
to the small tithe of corn
I'd placed in the shadow
of a Chinaberry tree.

Slowly with fledgling faith
she bowed her head to eat.
I watched her dine and contemplated
how much was lost in the race
to destroy earth only to own glass.

With the sound of a barking dog
our reverent connection was severed.
The doe turned and ran through
the few trees humans hadn't plundered.

When I could no longer see her
I lifted a prayer she would find peace
in the shrinking woods where
earth still whispers freedom.

# Tiny Acorn

Tiny acorn,
you are the seed
of a strong trunk
and reaching limbs.

You lie nestled in
earth's chilled womb
waiting for spring
to send its warmth.

Mother oak keeps watch
singing a lullaby of rain,
green sprouting and hope.

# The Breast of Primordial

Curtains of Spanish moss hang
from cypress limbs, tiny chains,
a living rosary, mysticism links.

They speak through the wind
pulling me into the heart of sound,
the urgency to listen to nature's
drum beat in my core, to hear earth write
my name in her book of genealogy.

I am the tiniest seed, the boldest heart,
the temporal human leaving her footprint
on the breast of primordial.

My scars seen and unseen sing harmony
with the bluebird weaving hope
through cypress and heaven.
Yesterday forfeits its knife to healing.

Baptized into the sisterhood of nature
I speak words of confirmation.
I am woman, freedom, the rose of Gaia, survivor.

# Hooded Priesthood

Mushrooms gather around
a decaying tree stump
like a hooded priesthood
joined in morning prayer
to petition God's mercy.

Distant thunder rumbles amen.

## Wildflower Seeds

Mortality is patient.
It's time stamp ending
waits for bones to surrender.

As my days grow shorter
I walk among the trees
eyes dry, heart open,
and listen to them sing
me back home to oak limbs
that taught me dreams
always bud in spring,
but winter is the womb
where they are conceived.

In the bold hours of daydreaming
I pluck wisdom from my scars,
write them into wildflower seeds,
and trust the wind to carry them
where tomorrow needs to blossom.

## Stained With Blackbird Wings

Morning stains the sky
with blackbird wings
carrying secrets pulled
from the summer moon.

Beneath feathered
oak limbs Trust sits
patient, still...
waiting for answers
to interpret questions.

What was, is, can be
gathers notes from
caged throats to place on
tongues bold enough
to sing of freedom.

# Faithful Watch

The tree's twisted eyelid
is my portal to the sea.
Mornings I rise to view
blue water sparkling
through leaf lashes.

There are days
I see a blue eye wink
of waves splashing,
others a cataract
fog of gray.

But with each sunrise
I smile and find peace
knowing my rooted sentinel
has kept a faithful watch
over me, the sand and the sea.

# Mother Spirit

Water is life.
Earth is heart.
Air is breath.

Mother spirit
I hear your redemption song
in the dancing drops
of the waterfall.

In my time of tears
you guide me to the white pine
where I breathe the scent of peace.

Comforted in the cradle of your heart
I drink light from the well of hope,
and lay my sin stones at the feet of forgiven.

# Light Play

# Where Butterflies Pray

Yesterday's cart of sorrows
disappears with the last evening star
as sunrise welcomes me into its halo
of psalms radiating a new day into my spirit.

Nesting where the butterflies pray
hope anoints my broken hallelujah
with the truth love still grows where thorns gather.

Peace sings in a bird wing choir
and I add my voice to the chorus,
*"Today is too swift with its hours*
*for my lips to only offer pain."*

## Sunrise

Sunrise needles
its cheek against
a lone pine until
frost spills its breath
to diamond morning.

Fingertips of light
find their way through
my window shades
turning shadows
into rainbows.

In the sacred hours
of unwritten my heart
communes with peace.
Worry is stripped of frenzy;
and prayer anoints my day.

# Deeper Blue

I swim through
yellow petal dreams
wondering if winter frost
will freeze my thoughts
to clouds stoning the horizon.

My sunshine stained hands
cut through waves of uncertainty
as my lungs struggle to expel doubt
after each breath of prayer.

Peace sits on the shore
waiting, trusting I will
not drown in the brine
of my questions.

The sky turns a deeper blue.

# A Hymn Note

I find God in morning dew,
in a crow's coal dust strut,
in clover dotted with honey bees.

Where the sun dances with the horizon
the gospel is spoken in blades of grass,
bass notes of bull frogs, a stream's diamond splash.

With each breath of wind
living stained glass reflects divine glory
as it gently directs me to an altar
where burdens lose their weight.

In my tabernacle of earth and sky clouds collect prayers
from my lips, and in the wing blush of butterflies I become
a hymn note in the hallelujah God writes across my heart.

# New Wings of Amnesty

Tomorrow pins its eraser
on the sun and I gather
all my mistakes around me
like wounded birds
waiting for new wings.

Watching for sunrise
to tap dance across
the horizon I feel today
run its fingers along my spine
drumming never at the
speed of chains.

Forgiveness begins to stir
my gut with trust renewal
is as close as my voice.
The lock of my self induced
condemning begins to bend
at the touch of the daylight key.

Heart humbled at the throne of error
I feel the weight of my wrongs
scrape my throat as they spill into
the collection plate of morning's amnesty.

# Four O'clock

Four o'clock paints its portrait
on my library walls in dancing leaf shadows
muting the turquoise of a flowerpot
feeding on shrinking sunlight.

It is that time of day when the unwinding
stalks my mountain of lists and chases
it closer to the corner of undone.

Incubated in the sound play
of jet engines and classical music
I let sundown into my breathing
and turn my eyes to contemplate
a white crane soaring in a picture framed sky.

Daydreaming with my fingers black keyed
to an alphabet I write the bird's flight
across a verse seeking wings not destination.

A roman numeral interjects itself into my reverie
as my gray cats stretch themselves toward dinner.
Walking the path of paws I leave late afternoon
to paint all my undone with the ebony touch of evening.

# Collecting Silhouettes

Have you noticed
how the sun
collects silhouettes
at dusk?

In the bright colored
dying of day wings pool
in ink spot flight,
leaves turn ebony,
and cityscapes charcoal
streets with shadows.

With the final pealing light
mortar, stone, blood, and bone
become a union of phantoms
pressed against melting wax.

# Bits Of The Moon

Bits of the moon fall
from a chalkboard sky
into cupped hands
eager to store wonder
in mason jars.

Giggles feed heaven
into glass as eyes twinkle
with firefly reflections.

Imagination, uninhibited,
sees God in light bearing wings.

# Twilight

Summer twilight dances
with shadow cloaked roses
to a sand song playing
on the southern breeze.

Void of sunlit demands
dreams wander
among blind windows
in search of hooded eyelids
to explore.

With a mother's tenderness
night hours stroke
a purring clock
in the calm before alarm.

Silently inspiration collects images
to feed poetry when first light
rises hungry for words.

# Hunger for Illumination

The light seeker
flutters on silver wings
around the bare lightbulb
on my front porch.

I watch the moth's erratic dance
and feel my spirit drawn to electric words
of hope, forgiveness, persistence.

A night's worth of crawling a mine field
of unfair disappears with the tenacious display
of a small creature's hunger for illumination.

## Answer Night

Answer night-
Where is the dream-
Where is the sigh-
Where is the nightingale?

Ah, said night-
Where is the beam-
Where is the cry-
Where is the sun's sail?

Whining sapphire, said the sun-
Where is the rainbow-
Where is tomorrow's heart-
Where is the morning glory?

Siblings, said the morning glory-
Where is destiny's bower-
Where is the gift of hours-
Where is love given sight?
Here-said Cupid's arrow-

## Dream Scent

A moonless sea
mirrors stars
chasing eternity.

Enamored with the glitter
I make angels in the sand,
and fill my lungs with
the dream scent of infinity.

# Mother Moon

So many tears rest on my tongue
waiting to spill grief across the horizon.

I sit beneath Mother Moon gathering
courage to step from my midnight quilt
into her arms that cradle agony
until legs are strong enough to stand on glass.

Weary unlaces my throat where I have
stored every word of doubt, and I set them free
to lay on Luna's hem where her light
restrings them into beads of peace.

# Night

Night puddles
under the oak tree
in broken stars and shadows,
the wind painting a Monet
with its branches.

In the distance an owl
recites a psalm to the moon
as I watch a falling star
burn its final light into infinity.

I sit motionless, reverent,
a soul listening, waiting for God
to answer prayer.

# Only So Many Lyrics

Nightfall drifts along my skin
in honeysuckle shadows.
I came to lament to the moon,
but the glory of wild vines
silenced my self-pity.

How could I beset such beauty
with a monotone of woe or
eclipse moonlight with complaints?

There are only so many lyrics
in a night song, too few for caustic rhymes.
Words chafed by grievance can't heal
a soul seeking deliverance.

Schooled by bloom and moon
I left bitter to silence, and filled
my throat with light to chase
away the demon of my moaning.

## Whippoorwill Song

Hypnotized by a velvet night sky filled
with dancing stars and whispered wishes
I listen to a whippoorwill sing of home.

I am miles from the gravel that dusted my toes
on barefoot summer dreaming, but when I close my eyes
I am a twelve year old with hands pressed to the moon.

In those yearning hours of child racing toward woman
love was hungrier, nights were longer, tomorrow
was close enough for questions, and hope never wore gray.

Blessed bird continue your chorus of innocence and winged
dreams.
I want to fly open fields where angels aren't concrete idols.
Whippoorwill teach me a new song of faith.

## When Shadows Grow Bold

In abandoned walls
where hope stores dreams
I collect words to armor
my spirit when shadows grow bold.

Dejected sheep dance
the world's ballet of bleak,
but I refuse to dance its choreography.

I will stand on my toes
to reach for stars.
Optimism never surrenders.
It thrives in midnight light
where the tenacious dandelion
breaks stone to bury roots.

# Weeds and Blooms

# A Day of Weeds

It is a day of weeds,
I am knee bent and
hands deep in a dirt
struggle with roots.

Gardening is supposed
to feed the soul, but
I am starved for reasons
why plucking thistle
will draw me closer to God.

Is it a lesson on being stubborn?
I dig deep in opinions until
I am barbed to denial I could be wrong.

I've been so busy growing louder
I've forgotten the wisdom in silence.

## Weeds into Whimsy

Silent tufts seed the wind
where sky and cloud
sort weeds into whimsy.

Floating as far as dreams
they seek a resting place
to defy impossible.

Soon yellow dandelions will
polka dot earth urging little hands
to tuck love into a bouquet.

# Dandelion Strong

I am moon, the northern star,
the wild woman gathering
mulberry shadows.

I am weed, dandelion strong,
growing where impossible
fertilizes the soil.

I am wild moon weed
turning shadows into star light,
a dreamer resurrected from killing fields.

## Flight of a Bouquet

A flower named weed
by science is magic
to a child who sees
her mother's bouquet
grow wings and take flight.

Beauty housed in
dandelion imagination.

## Beauty in Gray Sky Concrete

Tiny sunset blossoms
lace themselves to stems
bringing beauty to gray sky concrete.

In an urban forest of steel,
glass, and inhospitable
they are bright exclamations
nature hasn't surrendered
to the pounding anonymity
of blind spots.

# Morning Glories

Morning glories
cling to one another
on a broken fence
more crumble
than strength.

I reach for a blossom
awed by their persistence
to grow where hopeless
is homesteading.

The blue petals resting
in my palm ruffle in the wind
and I feel the courage in fragile,
the power to transform
bleak into beautiful.

Random, divine, karma…
all three, it doesn't matter.
Tuesday morning's lesson plan
guided me to discover the difference
between surviving and thriving.

# Wild Rose

Life places thorns
in the path of those
who dare to bud
in the drought of adversity.

Let your spirit become
a wild rose where impossible
is the perfect garden for blooming.

# A Jasmine Moment

Jasmine claimed the garden wall
in tiny spirals clutching brick and mortar.
The scent of the cloud of pearl white clusters
was heady, intoxicating, commanding.

On a street corner vibrating "don't linger"
a single Jasmine blossom caught my eye.
From a spring storm of a thousand perfume vials
I was enraptured by the arrogance of one
tiny flower's demand I pause and inhale its aroma.

In a sanctuary of seconds it was my Shaman
teaching me a moment of stillness has more value
than the foot chase to attain replaceable.

# Difference, Dandelions and Love

Climb upon the notes
and we shall sing a morning song.
You are the daylight in darkness
with your sunflower smiles.

Sing hearts that are different.
Sing eyes that bloom in dandelions.
Sing hands that reach with love.

Music wings will take us
beyond bullies, doubters
and definitions to open fields
where we can blossom as who we are.

We are the rainbow formed from tears
we no longer have to shed,
together we are a tapestry created
by coloring outside the lines.

Sing hearts blessed to be different.
Sing eyes that see the beauty in dandelions.
Sing hands that heal with the touch of love.

# Weed

I am more weed
than adored blossom
nurtured by a pedigree
of established roots.

My dandelion heart
finds home in the windswept
possibility of unknown.

With eyes to the sky
and ear to earth I gather
wisdom from seeds that
find a path to bloom
whether planted in drought
or abundance of rain.

# Knowing When to Bloom

Grass begs my knees
to kneel on green blades
growing in the intolerant
intrusion of man's footprints.

Humbly I rest my anguish
on a tiny piece of emerald
bold enough to survive
in the shadows of smog and steel.

In the vibrations of wheels,
voices, human motion,
nature sings of endurance,
hope, and knowing when to bloom.

Tears fall from my eyes
in rivers of solace.
I look at my grass stained hands
assured I'd touched my salvation.

# Spirit

# The World in Three Acres

When I was a young girl
revelation came to a small house
on a gravel road where agony
mossed the north side of dysfunction.
Angry words never reached
the roots of why ... They just
left the broken bleeding.

When bitter shrank the walls,
I ran to where the wild things go
and buried my tears among
cottonwood seeds.

With bare feet searching echoes
I roamed creek beds, watermelon vines,
and honeysuckle fences until a mockingbird song
bid me to sit and rest beneath its nest.

Open souled rhema came to me
in a psalm delivered on the wind.

"You are a child of earth and wings.
This world of three acres is your freedom.
Among decay, apple trees, bird,
deer, and rabbit are lessons to learn,
stories to tell, ties too strong to be severed.
The butterfly spirit lives in your heart,
wherever you fly hope will never desert you."

So many years have weighted clock hands.
In the gray of shorter days I still hear
the wheel crush on gravel where dirt road met destiny.

## Footprint Memory

Mud holding passages
in footprint memory
pull the DNA from
a Sunday afternoon stroll
to bind flesh and earth.

A sojourner's melody
hums through legs too young
to know the horizon is a
demanding seductress.

Tomorrow will always
hang its carrot from the sun.
New shoes can never erase
the footprints of those who
divided soul and yearning
into hours chasing it.

# Tempest

A butterfly secludes itself
on the belly of a leaf
when raindrops claim the sky.

With wings curled into security,
it trusts the storm is weaker
than the will to survive.

## Goddess of Small Things

I am goddess of small things,
violets on an oak table,
the rise and lowering
of window shades,
morning coffee,
handwritten notes.

My kingdom lies
somewhere between
sparrow and angel.

I have no need to measure crowns.

# Someone up There

When I was a child
I took my sorrow
to the sky.

Eyes and arms lifted
I danced my tears
around the sun.

I didn't know God had a name
or about being humble, or prayer.
I just knew someone up there listened.

## Until I am Cleansed Of Noise

I wasn't born with answers,
but questions feathering my tongue.

Why floats to a robin's nest,
the purple stain on lilacs,
a fox running along the fence.

A feral spirit in me
fights the flesh animal
I carry from mirror to street.

Horizons lure, rivers sing,
mountains flirt from
another valley I must cross.

A quiet voice whispers
through my bones urging me
to embrace silence until
I am cleansed of noise.
"Answers may lie on a stony path,
and you will need grace
to carry you where they lead."

# Home Has Found Me

Don't you want roots?
Everyone wants
at least one spot
of earth to hold
their footprints.

She answered,
"I don't want to settle
in someone else's dust
or follow a compass
that's lost its way."

She laid seashells
upon her wrist
and asked me
to listen to the ocean.

"When the waves stop
singing their song
of another shore,
I will know home
has found me."

# Wing and Call of Seagulls

Sea shells line the beach,
empty skeletons to souvenir
shelves with blue wave yearning.

I can't tell where the ocean begins
or where my footprints end.
I am one with water, sand, and sky.

The wing and call of seagulls
spirals above me in the anointing
breeze of salt and freedom.

The begging song I had written
with shadows lifts from my tongue.
I free my spirit to commune with joy.

# Healing

Standing where sunlight
polishes flood etched stone
I hear the echo of the Navajo
singing through the veins
of the Cathedral of Rain.

Slowly the voices search
the rooms of my agony
until they reach the
core of my tears.

Baptized in words my soul translates
I release my pain to the power of healing.

## This Poem Is a Blue Pool

This poem is a pool
This poem is vulnerable.
This poem is trust.

This poem is clear water
painted with sky,
rocks, and pine. It is as
deep as yesterday and
as wide as first sight.
This poem is a pool.

This poem is toes on
the edge gripping stones,
flirting with gravity,
wishing for wings.
This poem is vulnerable.

This poem is wisdom
that knows shifting earth
can be a leap into disaster.
It is a voice that brings
the rebel to the security
of solid ground.
This poem is trust.

This poem is a deep blue pool.
This poem is tempting fate.
This poem is wisdom inducing trust.

# Immortality's Feather

Peacock, the shimmer
trapped in your feathers
will not surrender to death.
The glory in your plumes speaks
of eternal gold and breath
reborn in lungs plague blackened.

Your eye feathers hold immortal's vision.
Life in blood, bone, and flesh sends hope
God will collect our dust to raise our bodies
from tombs hollowed by sorrow.

The majesty of your movement
erases doubt the earth you stride
can ever own the wind ruffling your wings.

Oh what is beauty if it is only defined
by a mirror that denies the glory of the soul?
Blessed peacock, you teach us grace
is the heart's paintbrush and our reflection
is an inward light no earthly artist
can translate to canvass.

## Cocooned In Wisdom

I am cocooned
in the wisdom
of my ancestors.

Whenever I need wings
the generational hum of survival
clears the storm clouds of my fear,
and I fly with the compass of my spirit.

Reborn from the stone path
of stout blood I rise with courage
and trust the seen and unseen
will not defeat me.

# Painted With Mortality

Hold love in the tender
hands of freedom.
If it chooses to fly,
give it room to use its wings.

No one can cage
the heart of spring
or demand affection
in the tumult of a hurricane.

Forever forgets the moon
is painted with mortality.
A broken spirit will mend
when it stops writing its obituary.

## Serenity's Voice

Serenity speaks...
Alone is the place to learn
the meaning of whole.

Kneeling among my scars
I find each sharp edge
of unforgiven...
and speak love until
I no longer bleed.

# Acknowledgements

I would like to thank Tim Malek for his patience and care in translating my vision for the cover image through his photography, and Jacqueline Smith for her work on creating such a beautiful book cover.

Scharleen Witt, you have been such an encourager. Your words have helped me push forward to completing this book. Thank you so much dear aunt.

Amber Jerome~Norrgard, the universe connected us so I could add another daughter to my family. Thank you for the laughs, the frankness when I procrastinate, and your love.

Charlie, Dawn, and Carrie, we are a crazy family full of joy, and love. I am so blessed to have been given such a glorious gift. Thank you for keeping the candle lit for dreaming.

# Biography

Susie Clevenger is an author, poet, and amateur photographer. She is author of the poetry collections, Dirt Road Dreams and Insomnia's Ink. Her work appears in the poetry collection, Poetry as a Spiritual Practice and online in The Creative Nexus, Poetry & Prose Magazine, The Global Twitter Community Poetry Project, Journey of the Heart, and The Yellow Chair Review. Susie resides in Houston, Texas with her husband, Charlie.

## Where to Find Susie

www.SusieClevenger.com

Like on Facebook.com: www.facebook.com/susieclevengerpoetry

Follow on Twitter @wingsobutterfly

Amazon.com Author Page: amazon.com/author/susieclevenger

## Other Works by Susie Clevenger:

Dirt Road Dreams
Insomnia's Ink

### *Collaborations with Other Authors:*

Poetry as a Spiritual Journey

Made in the USA
Lexington, KY
29 March 2018